J B Tajiri
Mortensen, Lori
Satoshi Tajiri : Pokemon
  creator

$28.25
ocn192079841
10/13/2009

Satoshi Tajiri

Pokémon Creator

Other books in the Innovators series:

Seamus Blackley and J. Allard: Xbox Developers
Tim Burton: Filmmaker
Chad Hurley, Steve Chen, Jawed Karim: YouTube Creators
Jonathan Ive: Designer of the iPod
Ken Kutaragi: PlayStation Developer
Stephanie Kwolek: Creator of Kevlar
John Lasseter: Pixar Animator
Shigeru Miyamoto: Nintendo Game Designer
Pierre M. Omidyar: Creator of eBay
Larry Page & Sergey Brin: The Google Guys
Burt Rutan: Aircraft Designer
Shel Silverstein: Poet
Frederick W. Smith: Founder of FedEx
Osamu Tezuka: God of Manga Comics

INNOVATORS

Satoshi Tajiri

Pokémon Creator

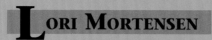

LORI MORTENSEN

KIDHAVEN PRESS
A part of Gale, Cengage Learning

GALE
CENGAGE Learning™

Detroit • New York • San Francisco • New Haven, Conn • Waterville, Maine • London

LIBRARY OF CONGRESS CATALOGING-IN-PUBLICATION DATA

Mortensen, Lori, 1955–
  Satoshi Tajiri: Pokémon creator / by Lori Mortensen.
    p. cm. — (Innovators)
  Includes bibliographical references and index.
  ISBN 978-0-7377-4269-5 (hardcover)
  1. Tajiri, Satoshi, 1965– —Juvenile literature. 2. Video games in-dustry—Japan—Juvenile literature. 3. Pokémon (Game)—History—Juvenile literature. I. Title.
  HD9993.E452T356 2009
  338.7'617948092—dc22
  [B]

                                                                  2008028249

KidHaven Press
27500 Drake Rd.
Farmington Hills, MI 48331

ISBN-13: 978-0-7377-4269-5
ISBN-10: 0-7377-4269-0

Printed in the United States of America
2 3 4 5 6 7 13 12 11 10 09

CONTENTS

Introduction. 6
Monster Innovator

Chapter One .10
A Natural

Chapter Two .15
Game Freak

Chapter Three 22
Pocket Monsters

Chapter Four .29
"Gotta Catch 'em All"

Notes. 38
Glossary 40
For Further Exploration 42
Index. 44
Picture Credits 47
About the Author 48

Monster Innovator

In 1962 a team of computer programmers at Massachusetts Institute of Technology (MIT) created the first computer game. Called *Spacewar*, this two-player game had two small spaceships called the Needle and the Wedge. Players scored points by firing torpedoes at each other while traveling through space. The pull of a nearby star's gravity could either reflect shots at an opponent or draw spaceships into it—and, then, destruction! It was the beginning of the computer game industry that would eventually produce such popular games as *Pac-Man, Donkey Kong, Super Mario Brothers,* and *Halo.*

As computer games grew more popular, some companies studied the top-selling games and designed similar games with the hopes their games would be just as successful. But the greatest success in the computer game industry did not come about that way. Instead, electronic game designer Satoshi Tajiri thought back to his childhood and created a whole new game he would have wanted to play.

The result was *Pokémon*—one of the most popular computer games ever produced and marketed. *Pokémon* was so successful it led to a television series, collectible trading cards, and movies such as *Pokémon the Movie: Mewtwo Strikes Back, Pokémon: The Movie: 2000,* and *Pokémon 3: The Movie.*

An **innovator** in the computer game industry, Tajiri received the Character Design Award in the Multimedia Grand Prix Video Game category from the Multimedia Content Association of Japan (MMCA) in 1991 for his Super Nintendo Entertainment System (SNES) software *Jerry Boy.* Six years later he received the Japan Software Grand Prize, the Computer Entertainment Supplier's Association (CESA) Award, and New Concept Award for his Game Boy software *Pocket Monsters.*

Pokémon Diamond and *Pokémon Pearl* were released in 2004 on Nintendo DS (Dual Screen) and sold 1 million copies within

The popularity of the Pokémon computer game led to three Pokémon films, including *Pokémon 3: The Movie*, shown in this movie still.

the first five days. In 2005 Tajiri created his first non-*Pokémon* game, *Drill Dozer,* for the Game Boy Advance. That same year, *Electronic Gaming Monthly* named Tajiri number nine on its list of the ten most influential people in the industry. Later, in 2007, Nintendo released *Pokémon: Battle Revolution,* the first Wii-Nintendo DS-linked title.

A Nintendo employee playing with the Nintendo DS. The launch of *Pokémon Diamond* and *Pokémon Pearl* for the new game system in 2004 led to the sale of one million copies in the first five days.

In spite of his record-breaking success, Tajiri is a soft-spoken man who shuns the media and the spotlight. This may be related to his diagnosis with **Asperger syndrome**, a form of **autism,** which affects social behavior and communication skills**.**

Today Tajiri continues to be a leader in the computer game industry as chief operating officer (CEO) of his own company, Game Freak. He explores new ideas and designs games that speak to his heart and the hearts of children around the world.

CHAPTER 1

A Natural

Satoshi Tajiri was born August 28, 1965, in Machida, Japan, a rural suburb of Tokyo. His father supported the family by selling cars for Nissan, and his mother took care of Satoshi and the house. As a young boy, Satoshi enjoyed exploring the forests, ponds, and rice paddies that were near his home. What captivated the boy the most were the insects he found. Everything about them stirred his imagination—from their strange appearance to the odd ways they moved.

"Dr. Bug"

Satoshi was so fascinated by insects, he dreamed of becoming an **entomologist.** As an entomologist he would be able to find out everything he wanted to know about the amazing creatures. But until he could achieve his dream, he collected as many different insects as he could. "Every new insect was a wonderful mystery," Tajiri once explained. "And as I searched for more, I would find more. If I put my hand in a river, I would get a crayfish. Put a stick underwater and make a hole, look for bubbles and there were more creatures."[1] Satoshi found so many insects, his friends called him "Dr. Bug."

Young Satoshi especially liked the fun and excitement of coming up with new ways to find and capture insects. At the time, children in Japan often captured beetles by placing drops of honey on tree bark. When Satoshi studied the beetles, he discovered they were active at night and slept under stones during the day. Instead of using honey, Satoshi came up with his own idea—he put stones under the trees. In the morning he removed the stones and found beetles just as he suspected he would.

As a child Tajiri spent so many hours playing video games he was actually given his own *Space Invaders* machine, like this one, by a local arcade owner.

As Tokyo and the surrounding communities grew, the forests, ponds, and rice paddies were replaced by highways, shopping centers, and apartment buildings. By the time Satoshi was in high school, his passion had changed from insects to playing video games at the local arcade.

Video Arcades

Satoshi spent countless hours at the arcade playing his favorite games, including *Space Invaders* and *Donkey Kong*, both designed by Shigeru Miyamoto. He spent so much time glued to the arcade games that an owner of a local video arcade gave him his own *Space Invaders* machine.

His unwavering passion for video games confused and upset Satoshi's parents, especially when he began skipping school to play. They were certain he was throwing his future away. "It was as sinful as shoplifting," Tajiri later reported. "My parents cried that I had become a **delinquent**."[2]

In 1981, Sega Enterprises, a popular video game manufacturer, held a video game contest. Sixteen-year-old Satoshi entered and won first prize. But this success did not calm his parents' fears about his future. At the time, there was no future in video games. Video game arcades were just hangouts for kids who had no future.

When Satoshi graduated from high school, his parents' hopes brightened. They encouraged him to enroll at a four-year university like other successful students. But Satoshi refused. Instead he studied electronics at a two-year technical college, Tokyo National College of Technology. After graduation his father offered to find him a job as an electric-utility repairman. It was a sensible offer since video games were still a little-known industry, but again Satoshi refused. He had his own ideas, and they all had to do with video games.

Once Tajiri took apart a Nintendo game system, he learned how to write the software that would work with it.

Game Freak

Although interest in video games was growing, little was written for the swelling number of dedicated players. In 1982, seventeen-year-old Tajiri and a few of his friends decided to write the kind of magazine they wanted to read. They named their publication *Game Freak* and wrote about secret tips and tricks and other techniques for winning popular games. Satoshi wrote each issue by hand, then photocopied and stapled the pages together. His friend, Ken Sugimori, illustrated the publication.

As the magazine became more popular, writing it by hand became too time-consuming. Eventually Tajiri stopped writing the magazine by hand and instead took it to a professional printer. Each issue sold for 300 yen, or about $3.00, and was about 28 pages long. The most popular issue was a special one about *Xevious* (*Zabius*). In this Atari game, players flew a combat plane over a scrolling landscape and racked up points by firing on enemy targets. This issue of *Game Freak* sold 10,000 copies.

The more Tajiri learned about various video games, however, the more dissatisfied he became. He was confident the games could be better. So he decided to design his own games. His first step was taking a Nintendo Entertainment System (NES) apart to see how it worked. Once he understood the inner workings of the equipment, he learned how to write the software.

Quinty

Five years later, in 1987, Tajiri produced his first game for the NES. It was released in Japan and the United States at the same time, but under different names. In Japan it was called *Quinty*. In the United States it was called *Mendel Palace*. The role-playing game, designed like an animated game board, became an instant winner. To play, players took on the identity of a character named Bon-Bon. Bon-Bon's mission was to rescue his girlfriend, Candy, from roving gangs of evil dolls who held her captive while she slept in Mendel Palace.

The game was especially challenging and required players to use logic and strategy to advance through eight dollhouses and 50 levels. Players could flip panels to crush enemy dolls or reveal a stash of secret weapons. Players who won were rewarded with an additional 50 levels of play. The media called it ingenious.

CHAPTER 2

Game Freak

In 1989 Tajiri formed his own game company. He called it Game Freak after his magazine and named himself CEO.

The formation of Game Freak marked the beginning of a string of successes for Tajiri in the video game industry. But most important, as he worked with Nintendo, he forged a lasting friendship with legendary game designer Shigeru Miyamoto, the creator of Nintendo's *Donkey Kong, Super Mario Brothers,* and *Legend of Zelda.* Thirteen years older than Tajiri, Miyamoto became Tajiri's role model and **mentor.** Tajiri memorized each bit of advice he shared.

Over the next few years, Tajiri produced *Jerry Boy* for Super Nintendo Entertainment System (SNES), *Yoshi's Egg* for Nintendo Game Boy, and *Mario and Wario* for SNES in Japan. The Jerry Boy character was so effective that in 1991 it received the Character Design Award in the Multimedia Grand Prix Video Game category from the Multimedia Content Association of Japan (MMCA). *Yoshi's Egg,* shortened to *Yoshi* in the United States, was a *Tetris*-like puzzle game featuring a green dinosaur character from another popular game, *Super Mario Brothers*. Players defeated the monsters and scored points by trapping monsters in between top and bottom pieces of Yoshi's eggshells.

In 1990 Tajiri also published a book with the Japanese Information and Culture Center (JICC), now known as Takarajimasha, Inc., entitled *Catch the Packland—Story of Videogames from Youth*. This book contained sixteen stories about Tajiri's childhood memories of playing different video games.

Game Boy Connection

In 1990 Tajiri saw for the first time an **accessory** for Nintendo's handheld Game Boy system that inspired him to design one of the most popular games in video game history. The accessory was a cable. Game Boy players used the cable to link their games so they could play against each other. "It was a profound image to me," Tajiri explained. "In *Tetris,* its first game, the cable transmitted information about moving blocks. That cable really got me interested. I thought of actual living **organisms** moving back and forth across the cable."[3]

That same year, encouraged by Tajiri's earlier video game success, Nintendo asked him to create a new game. Tajiri knew he wanted to combine the communication abilities of the cable link with the creatures from his childhood. "Kids play inside their homes now," said Tajiri, "and a lot had forgotten about catching insects. So had I. When I was making games, something clicked and I decided to make a game with that concept."[4]

Nintendo trusted Tajiri's instincts and gave him full creative control even though they did not fully understand his idea. Tajiri worked on the game for the next six years. Along the way his mentor, Miyamoto, provided valuable guidance and advice.

Two boys play *Pokémon*
against each other
by using a cable to
link their Nintendo
Game boys. It was this
interconnecting cable
that inspired Tajiri to
create *Pokémon*.

Monster Problem

Even with Miyamoto's help, developing the game was a long and challenging process. "The important thing," Tajiri explained, "was that the monsters had to be small and controllable. They came in a capsule, like a monster within yourself, like fear or anger."[5] Developing the game took so long that Tajiri barely had enough money to pay his Game Freak employees. When he revealed the company's rocky situation to them, five of them quit. Tajiri went without pay and only survived with the help of his father.

By 1996 the game was finally finished. But even after years of work, nobody knew if it would be a success. It had been a huge gamble that involved people's time, money, and effort. When Tajiri gave the finished game to Nintendo, he was convinced the company would reject it. Tajiri called his new game *Poketto Monsuta* or *Pocket Monsters*.

Tajiri's friend and mentor Shigeru Miyamoto (pictured here) provided valuable guidance as Tajiri was going through the difficult process of creating *Pokémon*.

Thing of the Past

The outlook for Tajiri's game was not promising. In the time it took to develop it, game technology had changed. More complex games with better graphics were now available that people could enjoy on their home computers. Game Boy's technology and simple images seemed like a thing of the past—as outdated as black-and-white TVs. Magazines, TV shows, and toymakers were not interested in the new game either. It did not make any sense to promote a game for a device that seemed destined for the electronic scrapyard.

In 1996 Nintendo released *Pocket Monsters* in Japan in spite of its poor welcome. The game came in two versions—a red version and a green version—and introduced players to 150 official Pocket Monster characters.

As expected, several months after *Pocket Monsters* was released, new computer games such as *Final Fantasy* rose to the top of the sales charts. But to Nintendo's surprise, because of a situation Nintendo had not anticipated, sales of *Pocket Monsters* began to grow.

While computer games were popular because of their advanced technology, most Japanese boys could not afford to buy those expensive games. But they had the money to buy the *Pocket Monster* game for their handheld Game Boys. They nicknamed the game *Pokémon*.

Pokémon Master

During the six years Tajiri had spent designing *Pocket Monsters*, he created a complex role-playing game that appealed to children like no other game had. At the beginning of the game, a player entered the Pokémon world and became a character that left

Pokémon monsters are kept in Poké Balls. The monsters are released when the balls are opened.

home to fulfill his dream of becoming a Pokémon master. Tajiri named the character Satoshi after himself. After selecting one of three Pokémon monsters, the character traveled from town to town earning badges by battling and collecting other Pokémon monsters. Each monster was kept in its own Poké Ball that the character kept in his pocket. When the character wanted to release a Pokémon from its Poké Ball, he reached into his pocket and hurled the ball into the air. In an instant, the Pokémon appeared in a blaze of white light. To put the monster away, the character opened the ball and the Pokémon returned in another stream of white light. When the character earned enough badges, he became a Pokémon master.

Tajiri increased the difficulty and excitement of the game by including a rival character the main character had to defeat at certain times before he could progress. Tajiri named the rival character Shigeru, after his friend and mentor.

CHAPTER 3

Pocket Monsters

One of the greatest attractions of *Pocket Monsters* was the wide variety of monsters, each with its own name and characteristics. Successful players memorized each monster's characteristics and figured out exactly which monster to match against another. Tajiri designed the monsters to fit into different categories. There were electric, fire, fighting, flying, grass, ground, ice, rock, and water Pokémon. As Pokémon won battles, they advanced to higher levels and evolved, or changed, into different Pokémon with greater powers.

Tajiri created the monsters' names by combining different Japanese words. Many players' favorite monster, Pikachu, came from *pika*, the word the Japanese use to describe the sound of an electric spark. The other half of its name, *chu*, came from the word the Japanese use to describe the sound a mouse makes. When the words were put together, the creature became an electric mouse.

Another monster, Nyoromo, was named after a characteristic of a frog. "It looks like a tadpole," said Tajiri. "There are little whirls on it because I remembered that when you pick up a tadpole, you can see its intestines because it's transparent."[6] Each of the monsters' names had its own special meaning. Tajiri's friend, Sugimori, who drew pictures for the magazine *Game Freak*, also illustrated the first 251 Pokémon monsters.

Pokémania

One of the most successful aspects of the game was Tajiri's decision to create two different versions. Since each one lacked about

One of the most popular monsters found in *Pokémon* is Pikachu, who has even appeared as a balloon in the Macy's Thanksgiving Day parade in New York.

a dozen monsters that the other version had, players who wanted to collect all the monsters either had to connect with someone who owned the other version or buy both of them.

Tajiri's addition of a hidden, secret 151st monster—Mew—ignited even more excitement about the game. Tajiri later explained,

> This was done on purpose. Mew was not originally in the games for people to acquire. You had to get it from interacting with Game Freak or Nintendo. You can't ever get a Mew without trading for it. It created a myth about the game, that there was an invisible character out there. Someone gives me Mew, then I give Mew to you, then you pass it on. Introducing a new character like that created a lot of rumors and myths about the game. It kept the interest alive.[7]

Tajiri's new game was so popular in Japan that 3 million games were sold within the first three months of its release. Its phenomenal success led to other products. Comics were published and the game's characters were developed into an animated Japanese television show. The show rocketed the game to even greater heights of popularity—more than Nintendo and Tajiri ever could have imagined.

Pokémon Shock

On December 16, 1997, something unexpected shook the Pokémon world. It happened during the 6:30 P.M. airing of the 38th episode of *Pokémon* entitled, "Dennō Senshi Porygon," or "Computer Soldier Porygon."

Twenty minutes into the episode, an antivirus program fired missiles at Pikachu and his friends while they were inside a

A scene from the *Pokémon* cartoon which caused hundreds of Japanese children to have epileptic-like seizures in 1997.

computer. Pikachu fought back with a thunderbolt attack that exploded across the screen with bright red and blue flashes. Although flashy explosions had appeared earlier in the episode, in this scene animators used a different technique called *paki paki*. The colored lights flashed across the screen like a strobe light, at a rapid twelve flashes per second. The effect caused young viewers to suffer from irritated eyes, vomiting, and **convulsions.** By 7:30 P.M., more than 600 boys and girls had been rushed to hospitals, and up to 12,000 children reported feeling sick.

News of "Pokémon Shock" raced through the media. When several TV stations replayed the flashing sequence during news broadcasts later that evening, countless other children got sick. The following day officials apologized to viewers, removed the show from the air, and banned its broadcast around the world.

A 1999 *Time* magazine cover shows some of the strange monsters found in the *Pokémon* game.

To stop future incidents they also created new guidelines about special effects that regulated the speed of flashing lights and how many patterns of lines, spirals, and circles could fill a screen. Viewers were also warned about sitting too close to their TVs.

Scientists later concluded that the rapid-fire explosions of light occurred at just the right speed to trigger **photosensitive seizures** in certain people. While most hospital visits were brief, two people remained at the hospital for over three weeks.

Even after this astounding incident, *Pokémon* sales did not slow down. Four months later the show returned to TV and developers created a hit feature film, *Poketto Monsuta*, that reignited the sale of Game Boy cartridges.

The game was so successful in Japan that Nintendo believed it would be popular in other countries as well. So in 1998 Nintendo decided to sell the game in the United States.

Two years after it was released in Japan, *Pokémon* hit the shelves and airwaves in the United States. Tajiri's game sold as *Pokémon Red* and *Pokémon Blue,* and TV stations across the country began airing 52 episodes of the TV show.

Name Game

Although Tajiri had created all the names for the characters and pocket monsters in Japanese, Nintendo changed their names so they would appeal to American tastes. Satoshi became Ash in the United States. Shigeru became Gary. And although some companies might have simply translated the monsters' names into English, Nintendo reinvented the names so they were just as clever in English as they were in Japanese.

In the Japanese version, the monster that looked like a salamander with a fiery ball on the end of its tail was called

Hitokage. *Hitokage* is a combination of two Japanese words that mean "salamander" and "fire lizard." In English the monster became Charmander.

The spotted green dinosaur with a bulb on its back was called Fushigidane in Japanese. This word was a clever combination of two Japanese words for "It's strange, isn't it?" and "strange seed." In English the monster became Bulbasaur. The water-squirting turtle called Zenigame, the Japanese word for "pond turtle," became Squirtle in English.

Nintendo did not change all the Pokémon names, however. The most notable exception was Pikachu, the most popular Pokémon. Its fun-sounding name captured its electric personality equally well in both languages.

Nintendo's strategy was a phenomenal success—*Pokémon* swept across the United States just as it had across Japan. People loved the rhyming chant of Pokémon names that closed each TV episode, ending with "Gotta catch 'em all." Sales of *Pokémon* were tremendous, especially when the company added another Pokémon tie-in—collectible trading cards.

CHAPTER 4

"Gotta Catch 'em All"

The Pokémon Trading Card Game was much like the video game. Players used cards that represented different Pokémon to battle each other and become Pokémon masters. Individual Pokémon cards included a colorful picture of the Pokémon and information and symbols about the character's strength and method of attack. The game also included trainer, energy, draw, and search cards. The card game became so popular that stores sold out almost as soon as the packs of cards arrived. Pokémon sales soared around the globe and became a worldwide **phenomenon.**

Interest in Pokémon surged again when *Pokémon: The First Movie* was released in the United States in 1999, earning $85 million by the end of its run. The star of the show was Pikachu, the cute red-cheeked Pokémon mouse that zapped enemies with its fierce electric shock as it cried, "Pika-chu!"

Nintendo developed other versions of the video game as well, including *Pokémon Yellow, Pokémon Gold,* and *Pokémon Silver.* These versions introduced players to hundreds of additional

Like the video game, in the *Pokémon* trading card game, players use cards representing different Pokémon to battle each other.

characters. Nintendo also released a battle-free version of Pokémon for younger children called *Snap,* in which players traveled to Pokémon Island and snapped pictures of shy Pokémon.

Also, two *Pokémon Stadium* games were released for the Nintendo 64 game system. Players connected this system to their TVs, so they could watch Pokémon battles in a large arena on a bigger screen. Then in 2001, Nintendo released *Pokémon Crystal,* the first Pokémon game made in color for Game Boy.

Banned from Schools

Pokémon's success eventually led to problems at school and home. Fights broke out. Games and cards were stolen. Children schemed to get valuable or rare cards by tricking kids who did not know any better. Some exchanged fake cards for real ones. At lunchtime, throngs of children played with the cards instead of eating their lunches. Many schools responded by banning Pokémon from school grounds.

People also complained that the Pokémon battles made the game too violent for children. But Tajiri disagreed. "I was really careful in making monsters faint rather than die," he said. "I think that young people playing games have an abnormal concept about dying. They start to lose and say, 'I'm dying.' It is not right for kids to think about a concept of death that way. They need to treat death with more respect."[8] In spite of the complaints and problems at school, however, Pokémon remained a global phenomenon.

Perfect for Children

As Pokémon swept across the globe, parents, teachers, and other leaders tried to explain its success. One doctor said that Pokémon appealed to children because they enjoy ordering and categorizing, and memorizing the characteristics of hundreds of Pokémon fit this mind-set perfectly.

Two young boys playing *Pokémon* in their living room. Critics blame video games such as *Pokémon* as being too violent for children.

A New York social worker offered another explanation. "After kids come up with a strategy to catch a Pokémon," she said, "they then have to train and nurture it as it evolves."[9] Experts admitted that few other video games appealed to this deep emotional part of the human personality.

Tajiri's friend and mentor, Miyamoto, offered another explanation:

> The biggest reason it has become that popular is Mr. Tajiri,
> the main developer and creator of *Pokémon,* didn't start
> this project with a business sense. In other words, he was
> not intending to make something that would become very
> popular. He just wanted to make something he wanted to
> play. There was no business sense included, only his love in-
> volved in the creation. . . . And that's the point; not to make
> something sell, something very popular, but to love some-
> thing and make something that we creators can love.[10]

Tajiri has his own ideas about *Pokémon*'s success. "When
you're a kid and get your first bike," he said, "you want to go
somewhere you've never been before. That's like *Pokémon.* Everybody shares the same experience, but everybody wants to take it
someplace else. And you can do that."[11]

Asperger Syndrome

In spite of *Pokémon*'s global fame and popularity, Tajiri remains
a quiet, private person. Some have called him **reclusive** and **eccentric.** Many believe these characteristics are a result of Asperger
syndrome (AS), a type of autism. While Tajiri has confirmed this
diagnosis, he has not discussed it publicly.

The **neurological disorder** was named for Viennese physi-
cian Hans Asperger, who published a paper about it in 1944.
The paper discusses a series of behaviors he had seen in several
young children in his practice. Although his patients had normal
intelligence, they repeated certain autistic behaviors and lacked
normal social and communication skills.

Many people diagnosed with Asperger syndrome, like the child pictured here, develop a skill in a specialized area such as computers.

One characteristic of people with AS is holding one-sided conversations. They often talk on and on about a single subject because they are unable to understand the expressions, feelings, and body language of others. As a result, many people with AS have trouble developing friendships. People with AS are also often absorbed in a single area of interest and develop an extraordinary skill in one specialized area.

While no one knows what causes AS, some experts believe **genetics** plays a part. Brain-imaging techniques have shown that the brains of people with AS look and function differently than normal brains. People with AS are usually diagnosed during the elementary school years.

Otaku

Tajiri is also known as *otaku*—the Japanese word for someone who shuts him- or herself away from society because of an obsession for the virtual worlds found in video games, anime, manga, or another interest. The word comes from the Japanese word *taku,* which means "home." *Otaku* refers to people who spend so much time absorbed in their passion, they hardly leave home. In addition to being socially isolated, otaku are also known for collecting things—the more the better—the central theme of *Pokémon.*

Winning Ways

Since the creation of *Pokémon,* Tajiri continues to work on developing variations of *Pokémon* and other games. "I sleep 12 hours and then work 24 hours," he once explained. "I've worked those irregular hours for the past three years. It's better to stay up day and night to come up with ideas. I usually get inspiration for game designing by working this schedule."[12]

A 2007 advertising display for the new *Pokémon* game developed for Nintendo's new Wii console.

His latest non-Pokémon game, *Drill Dozer*, centers on Jill, a thief who must get back her mother's valuable red diamond stolen by another gang of thieves. While many believe Tajiri's new games will never match the success of *Pokémon*, this idea does not bother the quiet game designer. Tajiri never created games to break sales records. All the games he designs are based on his love of the game and his desire to improve children's lives.

"I think a lot about kids," Tajiri said, "and what they need to make their lives better. You know, the cram school industry started when I was young. There was so little time to play. During school breaks, we'd run to the arcade to play games. Right now, there isn't much time for kids to relax. So I thought of games that could help kids fill those five or ten-minute gaps."[13]

NOTES

Chapter 1: A Natural

1. Quoted in Howard Chua-Eoan, et al., "Beware of the Poke Mania," *Time South Pacific,* November 22, 1999, pp. 62–70.
2. Quoted in Chua-Eoan, et al. "Beware of the Poke Mania," pp. 62–70.

Chapter 2: Game Freak

3. Quoted in Tim Larimer, "Interview with Satoshi Tajiri," *Time Asia,* November 22, 1999. www.time.com/time/asia/magazine/99/1122/pokemon6.fullinterview1.html.
4. Quoted in Larimer, "Interview with Satoshi Tajiri."
5. Quoted in Chua-Eoan, et al., "Beware of the Poke Mania," pp. 62–70.

Chapter 3: *Pocket Monsters*

6. Quoted in Larimer, "Interview with Satoshi Tajiri."
7. Quoted in Larimer, "Interview with Satoshi Tajiri."

Chapter 4: "Gotta Catch 'em' All"

8. Quoted in Larimer, "Interview with Satoshi Tajiri."
9. Quoted in Rebecca Segall, "Pokémon Craze Challenges Docs," *Psychology Today,* March/April 2000, p. 12.
10. Quoted in Richard Rouse III, *Game Design: Theory & Practice,* 2nd ed., Wordware Publishing, 2001. www.gamedev.net/reference/design/features/rouse1.

11. Quoted in Larimer, "Interview with Satoshi Tajiri."

12. Quoted in Larimer, "Interview with Satoshi Tajiri."

13. Quoted in Larimer, "Interview with Satoshi Tajiri."

GLOSSARY

accessory: Something that adds to the beauty or function of something else.

Asperger syndrome: A mental disorder that includes repeated behaviors and impaired social and communication skills.

autism: A developmental disorder marked by impaired communication and social skills and abnormal repetitive behavior.

convulsions: Strong involuntary contractions of muscles.

delinquent: Someone who fails to follow the law and do what he or she is supposed to do.

eccentric: Straying from normal behavior.

entomologist: A scientist who studies insects.

genetics: A branch of biology that deals with characteristics that are passed on through related family members.

innovator: Someone who does something new or solves a problem in a new way.

mentor: A trusted teacher or counselor or other adult.

neurological disorder: An illness of the nervous system.

organisms: Individual forms of life such as plants, animals, or fungi.

phenomenon: A remarkable event or extraordinary person.

photosensitive seizures: Disorders related to the brain that are triggered by flashing lights or unusual patterns.

reclusive: Seeking to be by oneself.

For Further Exploration

Books

Jan Burns, *Shigeru Miyamoto: Nintendo Game Designer.* Detroit: KidHaven, 2006. This fascinating book details the life of Satoshi Tajiri's friend and mentor, Shigeru Miyamoto, the most successful video game designer in the world.

Walter Oleksy, *Video Game Designer.* New York: Rosen, 2000. This appealing book explores the education and skills a person needs to become a video game designer.

Satoshi Tajiri, *Pokémon TV Animation Comic: I Choose You.* Minneapolis: Tandem, 2000. This graphic novel follows the adventures of Ash, Pikachu, and their friends Brock and Misty as they travel the globe on their quest to become Pokémon masters.

Web Sites

Official Pokémon Web Site (www.pokemon.com). This Pokémon USA Web site features games, songs, comics, and news about upcoming events and products.

Pokémon Games (www.pokemon-games.com). This is the official site of the Nintendo games series *Pokémon.* It includes news, history, and downloads.

Warner Bros. *Pokémon: The Movie* (http://pokemonthemovie. warnerbros.com/cmp/mainfr.html). This Warner Bros. Web site features news, games, and reviews of Pokémon movies.

INDEX

Ash (*Pokémon* character), 27

Asperger, Hans, 33

Asperger syndrome (AS), 9, 33, 35

autism, described, 9

Bulbasaur (Pokémon monster), *28*

Catch the Packland—Story of Videogames from Youth (Tajiri), 16

Character Design Award, 7, 15

Charmander (Pokémon monster), *28*

comics, 24

Computer Entertainment Supplier's Association (CESA) Award, 7

computer games, 6

Donkey Kong, 12

"Dr. Bug," 11

Drill Dozer, 8, 36

Electronic Gaming Monthly (magazine), 8

entomologists, 10–12

films, 27, 29

Fushigidane (Pokémon monster), *28*

Game Boy
   cable accessory, 16
   first Pokémon for, 31
   Yoshi (Yoshi's Egg) for, 15–16

Game Freak (company), 15, 18

Game Freak (magazine), 13–14

Gary (*Pokémon* character), 27

genetics, 35

Hitokage (Pokémon monster), *28*

insects, 10–12

Japan Software Grand Prize, 7

Japanese Information and Culture Center (JICC), 16

Jerry Boy, 7, 15

Jill (game character), 36

Mario and Wario, 15

Mendel Palace, 14

Mew (Pokémon monster), *24*

Miyamoto, Shigeru
  games designed by, 12
  as mentor, 15, 16, 18
  on *Pokémon,* 33
movies, 27, 29
Multimedia Content
  Association of Japan
  (MMCA), 7, 15

New Concept Award, 7
Nintendo Entertainment
  System (NES), 14
Nintendo Game Boy. *See*
  Game Boy
Nyoromo (Pokémon monster),
  22–23

otaku (socially isolated
  people), 35

paki paki, 25
photosensitive seizures, 27
Pikachu (Pokémon monster)
  in English game version, *28*
  in movie, *29*
  naming, *22*
  on television, *24–25*
Pocket Monsters
  awards for, 7
  development of, 16, 18
  success of, 19, 24
  versions, 19, 23–24
  See also Pokémon
Pokémon
  as nickname for *Pocket
    Monsters,* 19
  playing, 19–21

reasons for popularity of,
  31–33
success of, 7–8
versions, 27, 28, 29–30
Pokémon: Battle Revolution, 8
Pokémon Crystal, 31
Pokémon Diamond, 7–8
Pokémon monsters
  American names for, 27–28
  different versions of, 23–24
  using, 20–21
  variety of, 22–23
Pokémon Pearl, 7–8
Pokémon Shock, 26–27
Pokémon Stadium games, 31
Pokémon: The First Movie, 29
Pokémon Trading Card Game,
  29
Poketto Monsuta (film), 27
Poketto Monsuta (game). *See*
  Pocket Monsters

Quinty, 14

Satoshi (Pokémon character),
  20, 27
Sega Enterprises, 12
Shigeru (Pokémon character),
  20, 27
Snap, 30
Space Invaders, 12
Spacewar, 6
special effects, 25–27
Squirtle (Pokémon monster),
  28
strobe lights effects, 25–27
Sugimori, Ken, 13, 23

Super Nintendo Entertainment System (SNES) games, 15

Tajiri, Satoshi
as author, 16
awards and honors received, 7, 8, 15
characteristics of, 9, 33, 35
childhood of, 10–12
on importance of cable, 16
on interest in insects, 10–11
on Mew, 24
nickname, 11
on Nyoromo, 22–23
reason for creating games, 36–37
on Pokémon monsters, 18
on popularity of Pokémon, 33
on violence in his games, 31
on work schedule, 35

Takarajimasha, Inc., 16
television show, 24–27
Tokyo National College of Technology, 12
trading cards, 29

United States success, 27, 28

video arcades, 12

Wii-Nintendo DS-linked games, 8

Xevious (Zabius), 13–14

Yoshi's Egg, 15–16

Zabius, 13–14
Zenigame (Pokémon monster), 28

PICTURE CREDITS

ABOUT THE AUTHOR

Lori Mortensen is a multipublished author with more than a dozen books to her credit. Her books include early reader biographies about American heroes such as Thomas Edison, Harriet Tubman, and Amelia Earhart, and other exciting titles in Kid-Haven's Monsters and Mysterious Encounters Series. She lives in California with her husband, three teenagers, and a host of pets, including a ball python. To learn more about Lori Mortensen, visit her Web site at www.lorimortensen.com.